Cupcake Cookbook

Delicious Treats from My Kitchen to Yours

Linda Parker

introduction

Welcome, Dear Reader!

From the moment I baked my first cupcake, I fell head over heels in love with the process. The way simple, everyday ingredients could transform into something not just edible, but truly delightful, was nothing short of magic to me. And when I saw the joy these little treats brought to others, I knew I wanted to share this magic with the world.

Cupcakes hold a special place in my heart. They're bite-sized celebrations, individual portions of joy that make any moment a little sweeter. Whether it's for a special occasion or simply to brighten an ordinary day, there's a cupcake recipe that fits the bill.

In this book, you'll find my favorite cupcake recipes gathered over years of baking. From the classic vanilla and chocolate cupcakes that everyone adores, to the more exotic and gourmet flavors that will tickle your palate and challenge your baking skills.

This is more than just a recipe book. It's an invitation to create, to take chances, and to add your own personal touch to each treat. It's an encouragement to share these delights with the people around you and to create sweet memories along the way.

So, are you ready to preheat the oven and dust off your mixer? I promise, by the end of this journey, you will not only have an array of delightful cupcake recipes under your belt, but also a deeper love and understanding of the beautiful art of baking.

I'm thrilled to share with you my passion, my journey, and most importantly, my recipes that have been crafted with love, laughter, and a whole lot of frosting.

Happy Baking!

perfect cupcakes every time

---

8 tips for perfectly baked cupcakes

1. Ingredients at Room Temperature: Ingredients like eggs, butter, and milk should be at room temperature before starting your recipe. This ensures even distribution and better incorporation during the mixing process.

2. Sift your Dry Ingredients: Sifting your flour, cocoa powder, baking powder, and baking soda helps to remove any lumps and aerate the mixture. This results in a lighter, more evenly mixed batter.

3. Do not Overmix: Overmixing the batter can cause your cupcakes to turn out dense and tough. Mix just until you can't see the dry ingredients anymore.

4. Uniformity Matters: Use an ice cream scoop or a measuring cup to divide the batter among your cupcake liners. This ensures all your cupcakes are the same size and bake evenly.

5. Preheat your Oven: Make sure your oven is fully preheated before you put your cupcakes in. A properly heated oven ensures your cupcakes will rise evenly.

6. Positioning in the Oven: For best results, position the cupcake tray in the center of the oven. This encourages even heat distribution and helps the cupcakes bake uniformly.

7. Don't Peek: Resist the temptation to open the oven door before the minimum baking time recommended in the recipe. The rush of cold air into the oven can cause your cupcakes to sink.

8. Test for Doneness: Use a toothpick or a cake tester to check if your cupcakes are done. If it comes out clean or with a few moist crumbs clinging to it, the cupcakes are ready.

perfect frosting every time

7 tips for heavenly frosting

1. Butter Temperature: For buttercream frosting, make sure the butter is at room temperature, not melted or overly soft. This helps create a smooth, creamy texture.

2. Sift the Powdered Sugar: Sifting the powdered sugar before adding it to the butter helps prevent lumps in your frosting.

3. Gradually Add Sugar: When making frosting, add the powdered sugar gradually to prevent it from becoming grainy.

4. Piping Techniques: Practicing different piping techniques with different tips can elevate the presentation of your cupcakes. The simplest technique is to use an open star or round tip for a classic swirl.

5. Two-tone Frosting: For a two-tone effect, fill two piping bags with different colored frostings. Snip off the ends and place them side-by-side in a third, larger piping bag fitted with a piping tip. As you pipe the frosting onto the cupcakes, the colors will swirl together, creating a beautiful two-tone effect.

6. Frosting Consistency: The frosting should be stiff enough to hold its shape once piped. If it's too soft, try adding more powdered sugar. If it's too stiff, add a bit more milk or cream.

7. Exploring Different Nozzles: There's a wide range of piping nozzles available that can dramatically change the look of your cupcakes. Don't be shy to experiment with those and remember, the size and angle at which you hold the piping bag can greatly affect the final result.

cupcake baking glossary

Understand your basics

Batter: The mixture of ingredients used to make cupcakes before they are baked.

Creaming: The process of beating butter with sugar until light and fluffy. This technique incorporates air into the mixture that helps in leavening the cake.

Dry Ingredients: Ingredients that are dry, like flour, sugar, baking powder, baking soda, and spices.

Wet Ingredients: Ingredients that are liquid, such as eggs, milk, water, oil, and vanilla extract.

Frosting/Icing: A sweet, creamy mixture, often made of sugar and butter, used to cover or fill baked goods. The terms are sometimes used interchangeably, though icing is usually thinner and glossier.

Ganache: A mixture of chocolate and cream, heated and stirred until smooth. It can be used as a glaze, filling, or frosting.

Buttercream: A type of frosting made by creaming butter with powdered sugar. Varieties may include other flavorings such as vanilla, chocolate, or fruit purees.

Cream Cheese Frosting: A frosting made from cream cheese, butter, and powdered sugar. It's known for its tangy and creamy flavor, often used on red velvet and carrot cupcakes.

Whipped Cream Frosting: A light and airy frosting made by beating heavy cream until it holds stiff peaks.

Piping: The act of using a piping bag fitted with a nozzle to apply frosting, ganache, or other semi-solid foods to cupcakes and other baked goods.

Nozzle/Tip: The metal or plastic piece at the end of a piping bag that shapes the frosting or ganache as it is piped out.

Cupcake Liners: Paper or foil liners that are placed inside the holes of a cupcake tray before adding batter. They prevent the cupcakes from sticking to the tray and make them easier to remove and serve.

Zest: The grated outer rind of citrus fruits, used to add flavor to cupcake batters or frostings.

before you start baking,
let me tell you about...

Filling

If your recipe calls for filled cupcakes, here's how to create a hole for the filling. After the cupcakes have cooled, use a small knife or a cupcake corer to cut a small hole in the center of each cupcake, not quite reaching the bottom. Remove the piece and set it aside. Fill the hole with your chosen filling using a spoon or a piping bag. If desired, you can then trim the removed piece and place it back on top of the filling before frosting.

Frosting technique

Applying frosting evenly can be a bit tricky, but with a little practice, you'll get the hang of it. Remember, frosting is best applied when the cupcakes are completely cooled, to prevent it from melting.

If you're using a piping bag, start at the outer edge of the cupcake and work your way inwards in a spiral motion, then lift the bag straight up to finish the swirl. Applying even pressure to the piping bag is key to getting a consistent swirl.

If you're using a knife or a spatula, drop a dollop of frosting onto the center of the cupcake, then spread it outwards towards the edges. Be sure to have a good amount of frosting on your knife or spatula to avoid pulling up crumbs from the cupcake.

classic vanilla cupcakes

YIELD: 12 CUPCAKES   BAKING TIME: 20 MIN

Ingredients

1/2 cup (113 grams) unsalted butter, softened
1 cup (200 grams) granulated sugar
2 large eggs
2 teaspoons vanilla extract
1 1/2 cups (190 grams) all-purpose flour
1 3/4 teaspoons baking powder
1/2 cup (120 ml) milk
1/4 teaspoon salt
FOR THE FROSTING:
1/2 cup (113 grams) unsalted butter, softened
2 cups (250 grams) powdered sugar
1 teaspoon vanilla extract
2 tablespoons milk

Directions

1. Preheat your oven to 350°F (175°C) and line a muffin tin with cupcake liners.
2. In a large bowl, cream together the butter and sugar until light and fluffy.
3. Beat in the eggs, one at a time, then stir in the vanilla extract.
4. In a separate bowl, combine the flour, baking powder, and salt.
5. Gradually add the dry ingredients to the butter mixture, alternating with the milk. Begin and end with the dry ingredients.
6. Fill the cupcake liners 2/3 full with the batter.
7. Bake for 20 minutes, or until a toothpick inserted into the center of a cupcake comes out clean.
8. Allow the cupcakes to cool in the pan for 5 minutes, then transfer to a wire rack to cool completely.
9. While the cupcakes are cooling, make the frosting. Beat the butter until creamy, then gradually add the powdered sugar, vanilla, and milk. Beat until light and fluffy.
10. Once the cupcakes are completely cooled, frost them with the vanilla frosting. Enjoy

There's nothing quite like the simple pleasure of a classic vanilla cupcake. Perfect for birthdays, picnics, or just because, these cupcakes are a timeless treat that everyone will love. The soft, fluffy cake paired with creamy vanilla frosting is a match made in heaven.

decadent red velvet cupcakes

YIELD: 12 CUPCAKES   BAKING TIME: 20-25 MIN

Ingredients

1 1/4 cups (156 grams) all-purpose flour

3/4 cup (150 grams) granulated sugar

1/2 teaspoon baking soda

1/2 teaspoon salt

1 tablespoon (7 grams) cocoa powder

3/4 cup (180 ml) vegetable oil

1/2 cup (120 ml) buttermilk

1 large egg

1 tablespoon (15 ml) red food coloring

1/2 teaspoon white distilled vinegar

1 teaspoon vanilla extract

FOR THE FROSTING:

1/2 cup (113 grams) unsalted butter, softened

8 ounces (227 grams) cream cheese, softened

2 1/2 cups (312 grams) powdered sugar

1 teaspoon vanilla extract

Directions

1. Preheat your oven to 350°F (175°C) and line a muffin tin with cupcake liners.

2. In a large bowl, combine the flour, sugar, baking soda, salt, and cocoa powder.

3. In a separate bowl, whisk together the oil, buttermilk, egg, food coloring, vinegar, and vanilla.

4. Gradually add the dry ingredients to the wet ingredients, mixing until just combined.

5. Fill the cupcake liners 2/3 full with the batter.

6. Bake for 20-25 minutes, or until a toothpick inserted into the center of a cupcake comes out clean.

7. Allow the cupcakes to cool in the pan for 5 minutes, then transfer to a wire rack to cool completely.

8. While the cupcakes are cooling, make the frosting. Beat the butter and cream cheese until creamy, then gradually add the powdered sugar and vanilla extract. Beat until light and fluffy.

9. Once the cupcakes are completely cooled, frost them with the cream cheese frosting. Enjoy!

Red velvet cupcakes are a delightful surprise, perfect for Valentine's Day, Christmas, or any special occasion that calls for a touch of elegance. The rich, velvety texture combined with a luscious cream cheese frosting will make these cupcakes a hit at any gathering.

heavenly carrot cake cupcakes

YIELD: 12 CUPCAKES   BAKING TIME: 20-25 MIN

Ingredients

1 cup (200 grams) granulated sugar

1/2 cup (120 ml) vegetable oil

2 large eggs

1 cup (130 grams) all-purpose flour

1 teaspoon baking powder

1/2 teaspoon baking soda

1/2 teaspoon salt

1 teaspoon ground cinnamon

1/2 teaspoon ground nutmeg

1 1/2 cups (150 grams) grated carrots

FOR THE FROSTING:

1/2 cup (113 grams) unsalted butter, softened

8 ounces (227 grams) cream cheese, softened

2 cups (250 grams) powdered sugar

1 teaspoon vanilla extract

Directions

1. Preheat your oven to 350°F (175°C) and line a muffin tin with cupcake liners.

2. In a large bowl, whisk together the sugar, oil, and eggs until well combined.

3. In a separate bowl, combine the flour, baking powder, baking soda, salt, cinnamon, and nutmeg.

4. Gradually add the dry ingredients to the wet ingredients, mixing until just combined.

5. Stir in the grated carrots.

6. Fill the cupcake liners 2/3 full with the batter.

7. Bake for 20-25 minutes, or until a toothpick inserted into the center of a cupcake comes out clean.

8. Allow the cupcakes to cool in the pan for 5 minutes, then transfer to a wire rack to cool completely.

9. While the cupcakes are cooling, make the frosting. Beat the butter and cream cheese until creamy, then gradually add the powdered sugar and vanilla. Beat until light and fluffy.

10. Once the cupcakes are completely cooled, frost them with the cream cheese frosting. Enjoy!

Carrot cake cupcakes are a delightful twist on the traditional carrot cake. These cupcakes are perfect for Easter, springtime gatherings, or any occasion that calls for a sweet treat with a hint of nostalgia. The moist cake paired with creamy frosting is sure to be a crowd-pleaser.

decadent double chocolate cupcakes

YIELD: 12 CUPCAKES   BAKING TIME: 20-25 MIN

Ingredients

1 cup (200 grams) granulated sugar

3/4 cup plus 2 tablespoons (100 grams) all-purpose flour

1/4 cup plus 2 tablespoons (30 grams) unsweetened cocoa powder

3/4 teaspoon baking powder

3/4 teaspoon baking soda

1/2 teaspoon salt

1 large egg

1/2 cup (120 ml) whole milk

1/4 cup (60 ml) vegetable oil

1 teaspoon pure vanilla extract

1/2 cup (120 ml) boiling water

FOR THE FROSTING:

1/2 cup (113 grams) unsalted butter, softened

2 cups (250 grams) powdered sugar

3/4 cup (65 grams) unsweetened cocoa powder

2 tablespoons (30 ml) milk

2 teaspoons pure vanilla extract

Handful of chocolate chips to decorate

Directions

1. Preheat your oven to 350°F (175°C) and line a muffin tin with cupcake liners.

2. In a large bowl, combine the sugar, flour, cocoa powder, baking powder, baking soda, and salt.

3. Add the egg, milk, vegetable oil, and vanilla extract to the dry ingredients and mix until well combined.

4. Gradually add the boiling water to the batter, mixing continuously. The batter will be thin, but that's okay.

5. Fill each cupcake liner about 2/3 full with batter.

6. Bake for 20-25 minutes, or until a toothpick inserted into the center of a cupcake comes out clean.

7. While the cupcakes are baking, prepare the frosting. Beat the butter until creamy, then gradually add the powdered sugar and cocoa powder, beating until well combined.

8. Add the milk and vanilla extract to the frosting and beat until fluffy.

9. Once the cupcakes have cooled, frost them with the chocolate cream frosting and sprinkle with chocolate chips. Enjoy!

There's nothing quite like the rich, indulgent taste of chocolate. These decadent double chocolate cupcakes are perfect for those moments when you need a little pick-me-up, or when you're celebrating a special occasion. They're also a hit at children's parties, and make a great treat for a romantic dinner for two.

zesty lemon cupcakes

YIELD: 12 CUPCAKES   BAKING TIME: 18-20 MIN

Ingredients

1/2 cup (113 grams) unsalted butter, softened

1 cup (200 grams) granulated sugar

2 large eggs

2 teaspoons lemon zest

1 teaspoon vanilla extract

1 1/2 cups (190 grams) all-purpose flour

1 1/4 teaspoons baking powder

1/4 teaspoon salt

1/2 cup (120 ml) milk

2 tablespoons (30 ml) fresh lemon juice

FOR THE FROSTING:

1/2 cup (113 grams) unsalted butter, softened

4 cups (500 grams) powdered sugar

2 tablespoons (30 ml) fresh lemon juice

1 teaspoon lemon zest

2 tablespoons (30 ml) milk

Directions

1. Preheat your oven to 350°F (175°C) and line a muffin tin with cupcake liners.

2. In a large bowl, cream together the butter and sugar until light and fluffy.

3. Beat in the eggs, one at a time, then stir in the lemon zest and vanilla extract.

4. In a separate bowl, combine the flour, baking powder, and salt.

5. Gradually add the dry ingredients to the butter mixture, alternating with the milk and lemon juice. Begin and end with the dry ingredients.

6. Fill the cupcake liners 2/3 full with the batter.

7. Bake for 18-20 minutes, or until a toothpick inserted into the center of a cupcake comes out clean.

8. Allow the cupcakes to cool in the pan for 5 minutes, then transfer to a wire rack to cool completely.

9. While the cupcakes are cooling, make the frosting. Beat the butter until creamy, then gradually add the powdered sugar, lemon juice, and zest. Add milk as needed to achieve a spreadable consistency.

10. Once the cupcakes are completely cooled, frost them with the lemon frosting. Enjoy!

Pucker up, sweet tooth enthusiasts! These zesty lemon cupcakes are a citrusy celebration, inspired by the sun-kissed lemons of Sorrento, Italy. One bite and you'll be transported to a Mediterranean summer, no passport required!

matcha green tea cupcakes

YIELD: 12 CUPCAKES   BAKING TIME: 18 - 20 MIN

Ingredients

1/2 cup (113 grams) unsalted butter, softened

1 cup (200 grams) granulated sugar

2 large eggs

1 teaspoon vanilla extract

1 1/2 cups (190 grams) all-purpose flour

1 1/2 teaspoons baking powder

1/4 teaspoon salt

2 tablespoons (12 grams) matcha green tea powder

1/2 cup (120 ml) milk

FOR THE FROSTING:

1/2 cup (113 grams) unsalted butter, softened

2 cups (250 grams) powdered sugar

1 tablespoon (6 grams) matcha green tea powder

2 tablespoons (30 ml) milk

Directions

1. Preheat your oven to 350°F (175°C) and line a muffin tin with cupcake liners.

2. In a large bowl, cream together the butter and sugar until light and fluffy.

3. Beat in the eggs, one at a time, then stir in the vanilla extract.

4. In a separate bowl, combine the flour, baking powder, salt, and matcha powder.

5. Gradually add the dry ingredients to the butter mixture, alternating with the milk. Begin and end with the dry ingredients.

6. Fill the cupcake liners 2/3 full with the batter.

7. Bake for 18-20 minutes, or until a toothpick inserted into the center of a cupcake comes out clean.

8. Allow the cupcakes to cool in the pan for 5 minutes, then transfer to a wire rack to cool completely.

9. While the cupcakes are cooling, make the frosting. Beat the butter until creamy, then gradually add the powdered sugar and matcha powder. Add milk as needed to achieve a spreadable consistency.

10. Once the cupcakes are completely cooled, frost them with the matcha frosting. Enjoy!

Unleash your inner Zen with these matcha green tea cupcakes. Originating from the tranquil tea ceremonies of Japan, these cupcakes are a sweet whisper of the East in every bite. Get ready to match-a your baking skills with this unique recipe!

peanut butter delight cupcakes

YIELD: 12 CUPCAKES   BAKING TIME: 20 - 25 MIN

Ingredients

1/2 cup (113 grams) unsalted butter, softened

1 cup (200 grams) granulated sugar

2 large eggs

1 teaspoon vanilla extract

1/2 cup (125 grams) creamy peanut butter

1 1/2 cups (190 grams) all-purpose flour

1 1/2 teaspoons baking powder

1/4 teaspoon salt

1/2 cup (120 ml) milk

FOR THE FROSTING:

1/2 cup (113 grams) unsalted butter, softened

1 cup (250 grams) creamy peanut butter

2 cups (250 grams) powdered sugar

2-3 tablespoons (30-45 ml) milk

Directions

1. Preheat your oven to 350°F (175°C) and line a muffin tin with cupcake liners.
2. In a large bowl, cream together the butter and sugar until light and fluffy.
3. Beat in the eggs, one at a time, then stir in the vanilla extract and peanut butter.
4. In a separate bowl, combine the flour, baking powder, and salt.
5. Gradually add the dry ingredients to the butter mixture, alternating with the milk. Begin and end with the dry ingredients.
6. Fill the cupcake liners 2/3 full with the batter.
7. Bake for 20-25 minutes, or until a toothpick inserted into the center of a cupcake comes out clean.
8. Allow the cupcakes to cool in the pan for 5 minutes, then transfer to a wire rack to cool completely.
9. While the cupcakes are cooling, make the frosting. Beat the butter and peanut butter until creamy, then gradually add the powdered sugar. Add milk as needed to achieve a spreadable consistency.
10. Once the cupcakes are completely cooled, frost them with the peanut butter frosting. Enjoy!

These peanut butter delight cupcakes are a dream come true for peanut butter lovers. Perfect for birthdays, potlucks, or any occasion that calls for a rich, indulgent treat. The moist, peanut buttery cake paired with a creamy peanut butter frosting is a match made in dessert heaven.

raspberry almond cupcakes

Ingredients

1/2 cup (113 grams) unsalted butter, softened

1 cup (200 grams) granulated sugar

2 large eggs

1 teaspoon almond extract

1 1/2 cups (190 grams) all-purpose flour

1/2 cup almond flakes or peeled and chopped almonds

1 1/2 teaspoons baking powder

1/4 teaspoon salt

1/2 cup (120 ml) milk

FOR THE FROSTING:

1/2 cup (113 grams) unsalted butter, softened

1/4 cup (60 ml) raspberry jam

2 cups (250 grams) powdered sugar

1-2 tablespoons (15-30 ml) milk

12 whole raspberries to decorate (optional)

Directions

1. Preheat your oven to 350°F (175°C) and line a muffin tin with cupcake liners.

2. In a large bowl, cream together the butter and sugar until light and fluffy.

3. Beat in the eggs, one at a time, then stir in the almond extract.

4. In a separate bowl, combine the flour, baking powder, and salt.

5. Gradually add the dry ingredients to the butter mixture, alternating with the milk. Fold in the almonds.

6. Fill the cupcake liners 2/3 full with the batter.

7. Bake for 20-25 minutes, or until a toothpick inserted into the center of a cupcake comes out clean.

8. Allow the cupcakes to cool in the pan for 5 minutes, then transfer to a wire rack to cool completely.

9. While the cupcakes are cooling, make the frosting. Beat the butter until creamy, then add the raspberry jam. Gradually add the powdered sugar, then add milk as needed to achieve a spreadable consistency.

10. Once the cupcakes are completely cooled, frost them with the raspberry frosting and decorate with whole raspberries. Enjoy!

These raspberry almond cupcakes are a delightful treat perfect for a summer garden party, a romantic Valentine's Day dessert, or any occasion that calls for a fruity and nutty combination. The moist almond-flavored cupcakes paired with a tangy raspberry frosting will make you fall head over heels in love with baking all over again!

black forest cupcakes

Ingredients

1/2 cup (113 grams) unsalted butter, softened

1 cup (200 grams) granulated sugar

2 large eggs

1 teaspoon vanilla extract

3/4 cup (65 grams) unsweetened cocoa powder

1 1/2 cups (190 grams) all-purpose flour

1 1/2 teaspoons baking powder

1/4 teaspoon salt

1 cup (240 ml) milk

FOR THE CHERRY FILLING:

- 1 cup (150 grams) cherries, pitted and chopped

- 1/4 cup (50 grams) granulated sugar

- 1 tablespoon cornstarch

FOR THE FROSTING:

1 cup (240 ml) heavy cream

2 tablespoons (30 grams) powdered sugar

1/2 teaspoon vanilla extract

12 maraschino cherries (optional)

1 tablespoon of grated dark chocolate (optional)

Directions

1. Preheat your oven to 350°F (175°C) and line a muffin tin with cupcake liners.

2. In a large bowl, cream together the butter and sugar until light and fluffy.

3. Beat in the eggs, one at a time, then stir in the vanilla extract and cocoa powder.

4. In a separate bowl, combine the flour, baking powder, and salt.

5. Gradually add the dry ingredients to the butter mixture, alternating with the milk.

6. Fill the cupcake liners 2/3 full with the batter.

7. Bake for 20-25 minutes, or until a toothpick inserted into the center of a cupcake comes out clean.

8. Allow the cupcakes to cool in the pan for 5 minutes, then transfer to a wire rack to cool completely.

9. While the cupcakes are cooling, make the cherry filling by combining the cherries, sugar, and cornstarch in a saucepan over medium heat. Stir until the cherries release their juices and the mixture thickens. Remove from heat and let cool.

10. Once the cupcakes and cherry filling are cool, cut a small hole in the top of each cupcake and fill with the cherry mixture.

11. To make the frosting, whip the heavy cream, powdered sugar, and vanilla extract until stiff peaks form.

11. Pipe the whipped cream onto each cupcake and top with a maraschino cherry. Sprinkle with grated dark chocolate or chocolate sprinkles. Enjoy!

salted caramel bliss cupcakes

YIELD: 12 CUPCAKES   BAKING TIME: 20-25 MIN

Ingredients

1/2 cup (113 grams) unsalted butter, softened

1 cup (200 grams) granulated sugar

2 large eggs

1 teaspoon vanilla extract

1 1/2 cups (190 grams) all-purpose flour

1 1/2 teaspoons baking powder

1/4 teaspoon salt

1/2 cup (120 ml) milk

1/2 cup (120 ml) caramel sauce

FOR THE FROSTING:

1/2 cup (113 grams) unsalted butter, softened

1/4 cup (60 ml) caramel sauce

1/2 teaspoon sea salt

2 cups (250 grams) powdered sugar

2-3 tablespoons (30-45 ml) milk

Directions

1. Preheat your oven to 350°F (175°C) and line a muffin tin with cupcake liners.

2. In a large bowl, cream together the butter and sugar until light and fluffy.

3. Beat in the eggs, one at a time, then stir in the vanilla extract and caramel sauce.

4. In a separate bowl, combine the flour, baking powder, and salt.

5. Gradually add the dry ingredients to the butter mixture, alternating with the milk. Begin and end with the dry ingredients.

6. Fill the cupcake liners 2/3 full with the batter.

7. Bake for 20-25 minutes, or until a toothpick inserted into the center of a cupcake comes out clean.

8. Allow the cupcakes to cool in the pan for 5 minutes, then transfer to a wire rack to cool completely.

9. While the cupcakes are cooling, make the frosting. Beat the butter until creamy, then add the caramel sauce and sea salt. Gradually add the powdered sugar, then add milk as needed to achieve a spreadable consistency.

10. Once the cupcakes are completely cooled, frost them with the salted caramel frosting. Enjoy!

Dive into the divine world of sweet and salty with these salted caramel cupcakes. Born from the classic French tradition of pairing salt with caramel, these cupcakes are a sophisticated twist on a childhood favorite. Get ready to embark on a tantalizing journey where the caramel's sweetness is perfectly balanced by the sea salt's sharpness.

pistachio dream cupcakes

YIELD: 12 CUPCAKES   BAKING TIME: 20 - 25 MIN

Ingredients

1/2 cup (113 grams) unsalted butter, softened

1 cup (200 grams) granulated sugar

2 large eggs

1 teaspoon vanilla extract

1 1/2 cups (190 grams) all-purpose flour

1 1/2 teaspoons baking powder

1/4 teaspoon salt

1/2 cup (120 ml) milk

1/2 cup (60 grams) finely chopped pistachios

FOR THE FROSTING:

1/2 cup (113 grams) unsalted butter, softened

2 cups (250 grams) powdered sugar

1/4 cup (60 ml) milk

1/2 cup (60 grams) finely chopped pistachios

Directions

1. Preheat your oven to 350°F (175°C) and line a muffin tin with cupcake liners.
2. In a large bowl, cream together the butter and sugar until light and fluffy.
3. Beat in the eggs, one at a time, then stir in the vanilla extract.
4. In a separate bowl, combine the flour, baking powder, and salt.
5. Gradually add the dry ingredients to the butter mixture, alternating with the milk.
6. Stir in the chopped pistachios.
7. Fill the cupcake liners 2/3 full with the batter.
8. Bake for 20-25 minutes, or until a toothpick inserted into the center of a cupcake comes out clean.
9. Allow the cupcakes to cool in the pan for 5 minutes, then transfer to a wire rack to cool completely.
10. While the cupcakes are cooling, make the frosting. Beat the butter until creamy, then gradually add the powdered sugar and milk. Stir in the chopped pistachios, leaving a handful for decoration.
11. Once the cupcakes are completely cooled, frost them with the pistachio frosting and sprinkle the remaining pistachios on top. Enjoy!

Crack open the secret to a dessert that's truly 'nut' your average cupcake - the pistachio cupcake. This little gem, with its roots in the Middle East, is a delightful twist on the classic cupcake. Get ready to go nuts over its unique, rich flavor and charming green hue!

lavender honey cupcakes

YIELD: 12 CUPCAKES   BAKING TIME: 20-25 MIN

Ingredients

1/2 cup (113 grams) unsalted butter, softened

3/4 cup (150 grams) granulated sugar

2 large eggs

1 teaspoon vanilla extract

1 1/2 cups (190 grams) all-purpose flour

1 1/2 teaspoons baking powder

1/4 teaspoon salt

1/2 cup (120 ml) milk

1 tablespoon dried culinary lavender

FOR THE FROSTING:

1/2 cup (113 grams) unsalted butter, softened

1/4 cup (60 ml) honey

2 cups (250 grams) powdered sugar

1-2 tablespoons (15-30 ml) milk

Directions

1. Preheat your oven to 350°F (175°C) and line a muffin tin with cupcake liners.

2. In a large bowl, cream together the butter and sugar until light and fluffy.

3. Beat in the eggs, one at a time, then stir in the vanilla extract.

4. In a separate bowl, combine the flour, baking powder, and salt.

5. Gradually add the dry ingredients to the butter mixture, alternating with the milk. Begin and end with the dry ingredients.

6. Stir in the dried lavender.

7. Fill the cupcake liners 2/3 full with the batter.

8. Bake for 20-25 minutes, or until a toothpick inserted into the center of a cupcake comes out clean.

9. Allow the cupcakes to cool in the pan for 5 minutes, then transfer to a wire rack to cool completely.

10. While the cupcakes are cooling, make the frosting. Beat the butter until creamy, then add the honey. Gradually add the powdered sugar, then add milk as needed to achieve a spreadable consistency.

11. Once the cupcakes are completely cooled, frost them with the honey frosting. Enjoy!

Unleash the bee in you with these Lavender Honey Cupcakes, a sweet tribute to our buzzing friends. This recipe takes you on a journey to the South of France, where lavender fields are as endless as your love for cupcakes. Get ready to be the 'Queen Bee' of baking!

boston cream pie cupcakes

YIELD: 12 CUPCAKES   BAKING TIME: 20-25 MIN

Ingredients

1/2 cup (113 grams) unsalted butter, softened

1 cup (200 grams) granulated sugar

2 large eggs

1 teaspoon vanilla extract

1 1/2 cups (190 grams) all-purpose flour

1 1/2 teaspoons baking powder

1/4 teaspoon salt

1/2 cup (120 ml) milk

FOR THE FILLING:

1 cup (240 ml) milk

1/4 cup (50 grams) granulated sugar

2 egg yolks

1/8 cup (15 grams) all-purpose flour

1/2 teaspoon vanilla extract

FOR THE GANACHE:

1/2 cup (120 ml) heavy cream

4 ounces (113 grams) semi-sweet chocolate, chopped

Directions

1. Preheat your oven to 350°F (175°C) and line a muffin tin with cupcake liners.

2. In a large bowl, cream together the butter and sugar until light and fluffy.

3. Beat in the eggs, one at a time, then stir in the vanilla extract.

4. In a separate bowl, combine the flour, baking powder, and salt.

5. Gradually add the dry ingredients to the butter mixture, alternating with the milk. Begin and end with the dry ingredients.

6. Fill the cupcake liners 2/3 full with the batter.

7. Bake for 20-25 minutes, or until a toothpick inserted into the center of a cupcake comes out clean.

8. Allow the cupcakes to cool in the pan for 5 minutes, then transfer to a wire rack to cool completely.

9. While the cupcakes are cooling, make the filling. In a medium saucepan, heat the milk and sugar until the sugar is dissolved. In a separate bowl, whisk together the egg yolks and flour. Gradually whisk the hot milk into the egg yolk mixture, then return the mixture to the saucepan. Cook over medium heat, stirring constantly, until thickened. Remove from heat and stir in the vanilla extract. Let cool.

10. Once the cupcakes and filling are cooled, cut a small hole in the center of each cupcake and fill with the custard.

11. To make the ganache, heat the heavy cream until it just begins to simmer, then pour over the chopped chocolate. Let sit for a minute, then stir until smooth.

12. Dip the top of each filled cupcake into the ganache, then let sit until the ganache is set. Enjoy!

piña colada cupcakes

Ingredients

1/2 cup (113 grams) unsalted butter, softened

1 cup (200 grams) granulated sugar

2 large eggs

1 teaspoon vanilla extract

1 1/2 cups (190 grams) all-purpose flour

1 1/2 teaspoons baking powder

1/4 teaspoon salt

1/2 cup (120 ml) coconut milk

1/2 cup (120 ml) crushed pineapple, drained

FOR THE FROSTING:

1/2 cup (113 grams) unsalted butter, softened

1/4 cup (60 ml) coconut milk

2 cups (250 grams) powdered sugar

1/2 cup (40 grams) shredded coconut, for topping

Directions

1. Preheat your oven to 350°F (175°C) and line a muffin tin with cupcake liners.
2. In a large bowl, cream together the butter and sugar until light and fluffy.
3. Beat in the eggs, one at a time, then stir in the vanilla extract.
4. In a separate bowl, combine the flour, baking powder, and salt.
5. Gradually add the dry ingredients to the butter mixture, alternating with the coconut milk. Begin and end with the dry ingredients.
6. Stir in the crushed pineapple.
7. Fill the cupcake liners 2/3 full with the batter.
8. Bake for 20-25 minutes, or until a toothpick inserted into the center of a cupcake comes out clean.
9. Allow the cupcakes to cool in the pan for 5 minutes, then transfer to a wire rack to cool completely.
10. While the cupcakes are cooling, make the frosting. Beat the butter until creamy, then gradually add the powdered sugar and coconut milk.
11. Once the cupcakes are completely cooled, frost them with the coconut frosting and sprinkle with shredded coconut. Enjoy!

These piña colada cupcakes are a delightful treat perfect for a summer party, a tropical-themed event, or any occasion that calls for a fun and fruity dessert. The moist pineapple and coconut cupcakes paired with a creamy coconut frosting is like a tropical vacation in cupcake form.

tiramisu cupcakes

YIELD: 12 CUPCAKES   BAKING TIME: 20 MIN

Ingredients

1 cup (200 grams) granulated sugar

1/2 cup (113 grams) unsalted butter, softened

2 large eggs

1/2 teaspoon vanilla extract

1 1/2 cups (180 grams) all-purpose flour

1 3/4 teaspoons baking powder

1/2 cup (120 ml) milk

FOR THE TOPPING:

1/4 cup (60 ml) strong coffee or espresso (brewed)

1/4 cup (60 ml) coffee liqueur

1 cup (235 ml) heavy cream

2 tablespoons (25 grams) powdered sugar

2 tablespoons (14 grams) unsweetened cocoa powder

Directions

1. Preheat your oven to 350°F (175°C) and line a muffin tin with cupcake liners.

2. In a large bowl, cream together the sugar and butter until light and fluffy. Beat in the eggs, one at a time, then stir in the vanilla.

3. Combine the flour and baking powder, add to the creamed mixture and mix well. Finally, stir in the milk until the batter is smooth.

4. Pour or spoon the batter into the prepared muffin tin.

5. Bake for 20 to 25 minutes in the preheated oven, or until a toothpick inserted into the cake comes out clean.

6. While the cupcakes are cooling, combine the coffee and coffee liqueur in a small bowl. Brush this mixture over the tops of the cupcakes.

7. Whip the heavy cream and powdered sugar. Pipe or spoon this onto the cooled cupcakes.

8. Dust the tops of the cupcakes with the cocoa powder before serving. Enjoy!

Indulge yourself in a mini taste of Italy with these tiramisu cupcakes that are sure to have your taste buds shouting "molto delizioso!" Inspired by the famous Italian dessert, these fluffy treats are infused with rich espresso and topped with a creamy frosting - bellissimo!

peanut butter and jelly cupcakes

YIELD: 12 CUPCAKES   BAKING TIME: 20 MIN

Ingredients

1/2 cup (113 grams) unsalted butter, softened

1 cup (200 grams) granulated sugar

2 large eggs

1 teaspoon vanilla extract

1 3/4 cups (210 grams) all-purpose flour

1 1/2 teaspoons baking powder

1/2 teaspoon salt

1/2 cup (120 ml) milk

1/2 cup (125 grams) creamy peanut butter

1/2 cup (160 grams) strawberry or grape jelly (for filling)

FOR THE FROSTING:

1/2 cup (113 grams) unsalted butter, softened

1 cup (125 grams) powdered sugar

1/2 cup (125 grams) creamy peanut butter

fruit syrup or jelly for decoration (optional)

Directions

1. Preheat your oven to 350°F (175°C) and line a muffin tin with cupcake liners.
2. In a large bowl, cream together the butter and sugar until light and fluffy. Beat in the eggs, one at a time, then stir in the vanilla and peanut butter.
3. In a separate bowl, combine the flour, baking powder, and salt. Gradually add this to the creamed mixture, alternating with the milk, and mix well.
4. Spoon the batter into the prepared muffin tin, filling each cup about two-thirds full.
5. Bake for 20 to 25 minutes in the preheated oven, or until a toothpick inserted into the cake comes out clean. Allow the cupcakes to cool.
6. Once the cupcakes are cool, cut a small hole in the center of each cupcake and fill with jelly.
7. To make the frosting, beat the butter until creamy, then gradually add the powdered sugar and peanut butter, beating until well combined.
8. Frost the cupcakes with the peanut butter frosting. If desired, drizzle a little extra jelly on top for decoration. Enjoy!

Take a trip down memory lane with these peanut butter and jelly cupcakes.
Inspired by the classic sandwich, these cupcakes are a fun and nostalgic treat.
They're perfect for a kid's birthday party, a school bake sale, or just a sweet afternoon snack.

pumpkin spice cupcakes

YIELD: 12 CUPCAKES   BAKING TIME: 20-25 MIN

Ingredients

1 cup (200 grams) granulated sugar

1/2 cup (113 grams) unsalted butter, softened

2 large eggs

1 teaspoon vanilla extract

1 1/2 cups (180 grams) all-purpose flour

1 3/4 teaspoons baking powder

1/2 teaspoon salt

1/2 teaspoon ground cinnamon

1/2 teaspoon ground nutmeg

1/4 teaspoon ground cloves

1/2 cup (120 ml) milk

1 cup (225 grams) pumpkin puree

FOR THE FROSTING:

1/2 cup (113 grams) unsalted butter, softened

2 cups (250 grams) powdered sugar

1 teaspoon ground cinnamon

Directions

1. Preheat your oven to 350°F (175°C) and line a muffin tin with cupcake liners.

2. In a large bowl, cream together the sugar and butter until light and fluffy. Beat in the eggs, one at a time, then stir in the vanilla and pumpkin puree.

3. In a separate bowl, combine the flour, baking powder, salt, cinnamon, nutmeg, and cloves. Gradually add this to the creamed mixture, alternating with the milk, and mix well.

4. Spoon the batter into the prepared muffin tin, filling each cup about two-thirds full.

5. Bake for 20 to 25 minutes in the preheated oven, or until a toothpick inserted into the cake comes out clean. Allow the cupcakes to cool.

6. To make the frosting, beat the butter until creamy, then gradually add the powdered sugar and cinnamon, beating until well combined.

7. Frost the cupcakes with the cinnamon frosting. If desired, sprinkle a little extra cinnamon on top for decoration. Enjoy!

Embrace the flavors of fall with these pumpkin spice cupcakes. With a moist, pumpkin-infused cake and a creamy cinnamon frosting, these cupcakes are a warm and comforting treat. They're perfect for a Halloween party, a Thanksgiving dessert, or any autumn gathering.

espresso cupcakes

YIELD: 12 CUPCAKES   BAKING TIME: 20-25 MIN

Ingredients

1 cup (200 grams) granulated sugar
1/2 cup (113 grams) unsalted butter, softened
2 large eggs
1 teaspoon vanilla extract
1 1/2 cups (180 grams) all-purpose flour
1 3/4 teaspoons baking powder
1/2 cup (120 ml) milk
2 tablespoons (30 ml) espresso or strong coffee (brewed)
1 tablespoon espresso powder
1/4 cup (20 grams) unsweetened cocoa powder
FOR THE FROSTING:
1/2 cup (113 grams) unsalted butter, softened
2 cups (250 grams) powdered sugar
2 tablespoons (30 ml) espresso or strong coffee (brewed)
2 tablespoons of grated dark chocolate (optional)

Directions

1. Preheat your oven to 350°F (175°C) and line a muffin tin with cupcake liners.
2. In a large bowl, cream together the sugar and butter until light and fluffy. Beat in the eggs, one at a time, then stir in the vanilla and espresso.
3. Combine the flour and baking powder, add to the creamed mixture and mix well. Finally, stir in the milk until the batter is smooth.
4. Pour or spoon the batter into the prepared muffin tin.
5. Bake for 20 to 25 minutes in the preheated oven, or until a toothpick inserted into the cake comes out clean. Allow the cupcakes to cool.
6. While the cupcakes are cooling, prepare the frosting. Beat the butter until creamy, then gradually add the powdered sugar, cocoa powder, and espresso, beating until well combined.
7. Once the cupcakes are cool, frost them with the mocha buttercream frosting and sprinkle with grated chocolate. Enjoy!

Wake up your taste buds with these bold espresso cupcakes. Perfect for a morning brunch, a coffee-themed party, or any time you need a little pick-me-up, these cupcakes are a coffee lover's dream come true.

champagne cupcakes

YIELD: 12 CUPCAKES   BAKING TIME: 20 - 25 MIN

Ingredients

1/2 cup (113 grams) unsalted butter, softened

1 cup (200 grams) granulated sugar

2 large eggs

1 teaspoon vanilla extract

1 3/4 cups (210 grams) all-purpose flour

1/2 teaspoon baking powder

1/4 teaspoon baking soda

1/4 teaspoon salt

1/2 cup (120 ml) sour cream

1/2 cup (120 ml) champagne

FOR THE FROSTING:

1/2 cup (113 grams) unsalted butter, softened

4 cups (500 grams) powdered sugar

1/4 cup (60 ml) champagne

Edible glitter or sugar pearls (optional)

Directions

1. Preheat your oven to 350°F (175°C) and line a muffin tin with cupcake liners.

2. In a large bowl, cream together the butter and sugar until light and fluffy. Beat in the eggs, one at a time, then stir in the vanilla.

3. In a separate bowl, combine the flour, baking powder, baking soda, and salt. Gradually add this to the creamed mixture, alternating with the sour cream and champagne, and mix well.

4. Spoon the batter into the prepared muffin tin, filling each cup about two-thirds full.

5. Bake for 20 to 25 minutes in the preheated oven, or until a toothpick inserted into the cake comes out clean. Allow the cupcakes to cool.

6. To make the frosting, beat the butter until creamy, then gradually add the powdered sugar, beating until well combined. Gradually beat in the champagne until the frosting is smooth and creamy.

7. Frost the cupcakes with the champagne frosting. If desired, decorate with edible glitter or sugar pearls for an extra touch of sparkle. Enjoy!

Celebrate in style with these champagne cupcakes. Infused with a hint of bubbly and topped with a rich champagne frosting, these cupcakes are the perfect way to add a touch of elegance to any celebration. Whether it's New Year's Eve, a wedding shower, or just a fancy night in, these cupcakes are sure to make any occasion feel extra special.

classic strawberry cupcakes

YIELD: 12 CUPCAKES   BAKING TIME: 20 MIN

Ingredients

1/2 cup (113 grams) unsalted butter, softened
1 cup (200 grams) granulated sugar
2 large eggs
1 teaspoon vanilla extract
1 3/4 cups (210 grams) all-purpose flour
1/2 teaspoon baking powder
1/4 teaspoon baking soda
1/4 teaspoon salt
1/2 cup (120 ml) milk
1/2 cup (100 grams) fresh strawberries, finely chopped
FOR THE FROSTING:
1/2 cup (113 grams) unsalted butter, softened
4 cups (500 grams) powdered sugar
1/4 cup (60 ml) strawberry puree

Directions

1. Preheat your oven to 350°F (175°C) and line a muffin tin with cupcake liners.
2. In a large bowl, cream together the butter and sugar until light and fluffy. Beat in the eggs, one at a time, then stir in the vanilla.
3. In a separate bowl, combine the flour, baking powder, baking soda, and salt. Gradually add this to the creamed mixture, alternating with the milk, and mix well. Fold in the chopped strawberries.
4. Spoon the batter into the prepared muffin tin, filling each cup about two-thirds full.
5. Bake for 20 to 25 minutes in the preheated oven, or until a toothpick inserted into the cake comes out clean. Allow the cupcakes to cool.
6. To make the frosting, beat the butter until creamy, then gradually add the powdered sugar, beating until well combined. Gradually beat in the strawberry puree until the frosting is smooth and creamy.
7. Frost the cupcakes with the strawberry frosting. If desired, top each cupcake with a fresh strawberry for decoration. Enjoy!

Bring the taste of summer to your kitchen with these delightful strawberry cupcakes. Bursting with fresh, fruity flavor and topped with a creamy strawberry frosting, these cupcakes are a sweet and refreshing treat. They're perfect for a summer picnic, a birthday party, or any time you're craving a taste of sunshine.

caramel macchiato cupcakes

YIELD: 12 CUPCAKES   BAKING TIME: 20 MIN

Ingredients

1 cup (200 grams) granulated sugar

1/2 cup (113 grams) unsalted butter, softened

2 large eggs

1 teaspoon vanilla extract

1 1/2 cups (180 grams) all-purpose flour

1 3/4 teaspoons baking powder

1/2 cup (120 ml) milk

2 tablespoons (30 ml) espresso or strong coffee

FOR THE FROSTING:

1/2 cup (113 grams) unsalted butter, softened

2 cups (250 grams) powdered sugar

1/4 cup (60 ml) caramel sauce

Directions

1. Preheat your oven to 350°F (175°C) and line a muffin tin with cupcake liners.

2. In a large bowl, cream together the sugar and butter until light and fluffy. Beat in the eggs, one at a time, then stir in the vanilla and espresso.

3. Combine the flour and baking powder, add to the creamed mixture and mix well. Finally, stir in the milk until the batter is smooth.

4. Pour or spoon the batter into the prepared muffin tin.

5. Bake for 20 to 25 minutes in the preheated oven, or until a toothpick inserted into the cake comes out clean. Allow the cupcakes to cool.

6. While the cupcakes are cooling, prepare the frosting. Beat the butter until creamy, then gradually add the powdered sugar, beating until well combined. Stir in the caramel sauce until the frosting is smooth and creamy.

7. Once the cupcakes are cool, frost them with the caramel frosting. Drizzle a little extra caramel sauce on top for decoration if desired. Enjoy!

Start your day off with a buzz (and a sugar rush) with these irresistible caramel macchiato cupcakes. With a delicate coffee-infused cake and creamy caramel frosting, these little treats will have you feeling like you're sipping on your favorite Starbucks drink in cupcake form.

mint chocolate cupcakes

YIELD: 12 CUPCAKES   BAKING TIME: 20-25 MIN

Ingredients

1/2 cup (113 grams) unsalted butter, softened
1 cup (200 grams) granulated sugar
2 large eggs
1 teaspoon vanilla extract
1 3/4 cups (210 grams) all-purpose flour
1/2 cup (45 grams) unsweetened cocoa powder
1 1/2 teaspoons baking powder
1/4 teaspoon baking soda
1/4 teaspoon salt
1 cup (240 ml) milk
FOR THE FROSTING:
1/2 cup (113 grams) unsalted butter, softened
4 cups (500 grams) powdered sugar
1/4 teaspoon mint extract
2-3 drops green food coloring (optional)

Directions

1. Preheat your oven to 350°F (175°C) and line a muffin tin with cupcake liners.
2. In a large bowl, cream together the butter and sugar until light and fluffy. Beat in the eggs, one at a time, then stir in the vanilla.
3. In a separate bowl, combine the flour, cocoa powder, baking powder, baking soda, and salt. Gradually add this to the creamed mixture, alternating with the milk, and mix well.
4. Spoon the batter into the prepared muffin tin, filling each cup about two-thirds full.
5. Bake for 20 to 25 minutes in the preheated oven, or until a toothpick inserted into the cake comes out clean. Allow the cupcakes to cool.
6. To make the frosting, beat the butter until creamy, then gradually add the powdered sugar, beating until well combined. Beat in the mint extract and food coloring, if using, until the frosting is smooth and creamy.
7. Frost the cupcakes with the mint frosting. If desired, sprinkle with chocolate shavings or mini chocolate chips for decoration. Enjoy!

Legend has it, this recipe was born when a Swiss chocolatier accidentally dropped a mint leaf into his chocolate mix, creating a serendipitous blend that's been a sensation ever since. Get ready to embark on a culinary adventure that's minty, chocolaty, and absolutely irresistible!

coconut cupcakes

YIELD: 12 CUPCAKES   BAKING TIME: 20-25 MIN

Ingredients

1/2 cup (113 grams) unsalted butter, softened

1 cup (200 grams) granulated sugar

2 large eggs

1 teaspoon vanilla extract

1 3/4 cups (210 grams) all-purpose flour

1 1/2 teaspoons baking powder

1/4 teaspoon baking soda

1/4 teaspoon salt

1/2 cup (120 ml) coconut milk

1/2 cup (40 grams) shredded coconut

FOR THE FROSTING:

1/2 cup (113 grams) unsalted butter, softened

4 cups (500 grams) powdered sugar

1/4 cup (60 ml) coconut milk

1/2 cup (40 grams) shredded coconut (for decoration)

Directions

1. Preheat your oven to 350°F (175°C) and line a muffin tin with cupcake liners.

2. In a large bowl, cream together the butter and sugar until light and fluffy. Beat in the eggs, one at a time, then stir in the vanilla.

3. In a separate bowl, combine the flour, baking powder, baking soda, and salt. Gradually add this to the creamed mixture, alternating with the coconut milk, and mix well. Fold in the shredded coconut.

4. Spoon the batter into the prepared muffin tin, filling each cup about two-thirds full.

5. Bake for 20 to 25 minutes in the preheated oven, or until a toothpick inserted into the cake comes out clean. Allow the cupcakes to cool.

6. To make the frosting, beat the butter until creamy, then gradually add the powdered sugar, beating until well combined. Gradually beat in the coconut milk until the frosting is smooth and creamy.

7. Frost the cupcakes with the coconut frosting. Sprinkle the tops with shredded coconut for decoration. Enjoy!

Escape to a tropical paradise with these coconut cupcakes. With a moist, coconut-infused cake and a creamy coconut frosting, these cupcakes are a coconut lover's dream. They're perfect for a summer barbecue, a beach-themed party, or any time you're craving a taste of the tropics.

chai spice cupcakes

YIELD: 12 CUPCAKES   BAKING TIME: 20 - 25 MIN

Ingredients

1/2 cup (113 grams) unsalted butter, softened
1 cup (200 grams) granulated sugar
2 large eggs
1 teaspoon vanilla extract
1 3/4 cups (210 grams) all-purpose flour
1 1/2 teaspoons baking powder
1/4 teaspoon baking soda
1/4 teaspoon salt
1/2 teaspoon ground cinnamon
1/2 teaspoon ground ginger
1/4 teaspoon ground cardamom
1/4 teaspoon ground cloves
1/4 teaspoon ground nutmeg
1 cup (240 ml) milk
FOR THE FROSTING:
1/2 cup (113 grams) unsalted butter, softened
4 cups (500 grams) powdered sugar
1/4 teaspoon ground cinnamon
1/4 teaspoon ground ginger
1/8 teaspoon ground cardamom
1/8 teaspoon ground cloves
1/8 teaspoon ground nutmeg
30 ml milk

Directions

1. Preheat your oven to 350°F (175°C) and line a muffin tin with cupcake liners.
2. In a large bowl, cream together the butter and sugar until light and fluffy. Beat in the eggs, one at a time, then stir in the vanilla.
3. In a separate bowl, combine the flour, baking powder, baking soda, salt, and spices. Gradually add this to the creamed mixture, alternating with the milk, and mix well.
4. Spoon the batter into the prepared muffin tin, filling each cup about two-thirds full.
5. Bake for 20 to 25 minutes in the preheated oven, or until a toothpick inserted into the cake comes out clean. Allow the cupcakes to cool.
6. To make the frosting, beat the butter until creamy, then gradually add the powdered sugar and spices, beating until well combined. Gradually beat in the milk until the frosting is smooth and creamy.
7. Frost the cupcakes with the chai spice frosting. If desired, sprinkle a little extra cinnamon on top for decoration. Enjoy!

cotton candy cupcakes

YIELD: 12 CUPCAKES   BAKING TIME: 20 MIN

Ingredients

1 1/2 cups (190 grams) all-purpose flour

1 1/2 teaspoons baking powder

1/4 teaspoon salt

1/2 cup (113 grams) unsalted butter, softened

1 cup (200 grams) granulated sugar

2 large eggs

2 teaspoons vanilla extract

1/2 cup (120 ml) whole milk

1/2 cup (20 grams) cotton candy, finely chopped

Pink and blue food coloring (optional)

FOR THE COTTON CANDY FROSTING:

1 cup (226 grams) unsalted butter, softened

4 cups (500 grams) powdered sugar

2 teaspoons vanilla extract

2 tablespoons (30 ml) whole milk

1/2 cup (20 grams) cotton candy, finely chopped

Pink and blue food coloring (optional)

Directions

1. Preheat your oven to 350°F (175°C) and line a muffin tin with cupcake liners.

2. In a medium bowl, whisk together the flour, baking powder, and salt.

3. In a large bowl, beat the butter and sugar together until light and fluffy. Beat in the eggs, one at a time, then stir in the vanilla extract.

4. Gradually mix in the dry ingredients, alternating with the milk, beginning and ending with the dry ingredients. Stir in the chopped cotton candy.

5. If desired, divide the batter between two bowls and tint one pink and the other blue. Spoon the batter into the cupcake liners, filling each about 2/3 full.

6. Bake for 20 minutes, or until a toothpick inserted into the center of a cupcake comes out clean. Allow the cupcakes to cool in the pan for 5 minutes, then transfer them to a wire rack to cool completely.

7. While the cupcakes are cooling, make the frosting. Beat the butter until creamy, then gradually beat in the powdered sugar. Stir in the vanilla extract and milk, then fold in the chopped cotton candy.

8. If desired, divide the frosting between two bowls and tint one pink and the other blue. For the two-tone icing, read the 'perfect frosting every time' section at the beginning of this book for instructions. Or simply decorate some cupcakes using blue frosting and some using pink frosting!

apple pie cupcakes

YIELD: 12 CUPCAKES   BAKING TIME: 20-25 MIN

Ingredients

1 1/2 cups (190 grams) all-purpose flour

1 1/2 teaspoons baking powder

1/2 teaspoon salt

2 teaspoons cinnamon

1/2 teaspoon nutmeg

1/2 cup (113 grams) unsalted butter, at room temperature

1 cup (200 grams) granulated sugar

2 large eggs

1 teaspoon pure vanilla extract

3/4 cup (180 ml) milk

2 cups (300 grams) peeled, cored and chopped fresh apples

FOR THE FROSTING:

1/2 cup (113 grams) unsalted butter, at room temperature

4 cups (500 grams) powdered sugar

2 teaspoons vanilla extract

2-4 tablespoons milk

Directions

1. Preheat your oven to 350°F (175°C) and line a muffin tin with cupcake liners.
2. In a medium bowl, whisk together the flour, baking powder, salt, cinnamon, and nutmeg.
3. In a large bowl, beat the butter and sugar together until light and fluffy. Beat in the eggs, one at a time, followed by the vanilla extract.
4. Gradually add the dry ingredients to the butter mixture, alternating with the milk, beginning and ending with the dry ingredients. Stir in the chopped apples. The size of your apple chunks is entirely up to you, feel free to experiment with bigger chunks or grate your apples for more uniform cupcake texture.
5. Divide the batter evenly among the cupcake liners and bake for 20-25 minutes, or until a toothpick inserted into the center of a cupcake comes out clean.
6. While the cupcakes are cooling, make the frosting. Beat the butter until creamy, then gradually add the powdered sugar, vanilla extract, and enough milk to achieve a spreadable consistency.
7. Once the cupcakes are completely cool, frost them with the vanilla frosting.

There's nothing quite like the taste of a fresh apple pie, especially when it's baked into a cupcake! These apple pie cupcakes are the perfect treat for a crisp fall day, a family gathering, or just because you're in the mood for something sweet and comforting.

butterscotch bliss cupcakes

YIELD: 12 CUPCAKES   BAKING TIME: 20 MIN

Ingredients

1/2 cup (113 grams) unsalted butter

1 cup (200 grams) brown sugar

2 large eggs

1 teaspoon vanilla extract

1 1/2 cups (190 grams) all-purpose flour

1 1/2 teaspoons baking powder

1/4 teaspoon salt

1/2 cup (120 ml) milk

1/2 cup (120 grams) butterscotch chips

FOR THE BUTTERSCOTCH FROSTING:

1/2 cup (113 grams) unsalted butter

1 cup (200 grams) brown sugar

1/4 cup (60 ml) milk

2 cups (250 grams) powdered sugar

Directions

1. Preheat your oven to 350°F (175°C) and line a muffin tin with cupcake liners.

2. In a large bowl, cream together the butter and brown sugar until light and fluffy.

3. Beat in the eggs one at a time, followed by the vanilla extract.

4. In a separate bowl, combine the flour, baking powder, and salt.

5. Gradually add the dry ingredients to the butter mixture, alternating with the milk. Stir until just combined.

6. Fold in the butterscotch chips.

7. Divide the batter evenly among the cupcake liners and bake for 20 minutes, or until a toothpick inserted into the center comes out clean.

8. While the cupcakes are cooling, make the frosting. Melt the butter in a saucepan over medium heat. Add the brown sugar and milk, stirring until the sugar has completely dissolved.

9. Remove from heat and let cool for a few minutes. Gradually whisk in the powdered sugar until the frosting is smooth and creamy.

10. Once the cupcakes are completely cooled, frost them with the butterscotch frosting. Enjoy!

Butterscotch cupcakes, a sweet nod to the old-fashioned candy, are here to take your taste buds on a nostalgic journey. Born from the marriage of butter and brown sugar, these cupcakes are a testament to the fact that sometimes, the simplest ingredients create the most extraordinary flavors.

cinnamon roll cupcakes

YIELD: 12 CUPCAKES   BAKING TIME: 20 MIN

Ingredients

1 1/2 cups (190 grams) all-purpose flour

1 1/2 teaspoons baking powder

1/2 teaspoon salt

1 teaspoon cinnamon

1/2 cup (113 grams) unsalted butter, softened

1 cup (200 grams) granulated sugar

2 large eggs

2 teaspoons vanilla extract

3/4 cup (180 ml) milk

FOR THE CINNAMON SWIRL:

1/4 cup (50 grams) brown sugar

1 tablespoon ground cinnamon

FOR THE ICING:

1 cup (125 grams) powdered sugar

2 tablespoons milk

Directions

1. Preheat your oven to 350°F (175°C) and line a muffin tin with cupcake liners.

2. In a medium bowl, whisk together the flour, baking powder, salt, and cinnamon.

3. In a large bowl, beat the butter and sugar together until light and fluffy. Beat in the eggs one at a time, then stir in the vanilla.

4. Gradually mix in the dry ingredients and milk, alternating between the two, beginning and ending with the dry ingredients.

5. In a small bowl, mix together the brown sugar and cinnamon for the cinnamon swirl.

6. Fill each cupcake liner about 1/3 full with the cupcake batter. Sprinkle a layer of the cinnamon sugar mixture over the batter, then top with more batter until the liners are about 2/3 full.

7. Bake for 20 minutes, or until a toothpick inserted into the center of a cupcake comes out clean.

8. While the cupcakes are cooling, whisk together the powdered sugar and milk to make the icing. Drizzle the icing over the cooled cupcakes.

9. Enjoy your cinnamon roll cupcakes warm, just like a fresh cinnamon roll!

There's nothing quite like the aroma of cinnamon rolls baking in the oven. Now, imagine that same comforting scent wafting from your oven, but in cupcake form! These cinnamon roll cupcakes are the perfect treat for a cozy Sunday brunch or a festive holiday gathering. They're a delightful twist on the classic cinnamon roll, and they're sure to impress your guests.

mint oreo cupcakes

YIELD: 12 CUPCAKES   BAKING TIME: 20 MIN

Ingredients

1 1/2 cups (190 grams) all-purpose flour

1/2 cup (45 grams) unsweetened cocoa powder

1 1/4 cups (250 grams) granulated sugar

1/2 teaspoon baking powder

1/2 teaspoon baking soda

1/2 teaspoon salt

2 large eggs

1/2 cup (120 ml) whole milk

1/2 cup (120 ml) vegetable oil

2 teaspoons vanilla extract

1/2 teaspoon mint extract

12 Oreos, crushed

FOR THE FROSTING:

1/2 cup (115 grams) unsalted butter, softened

2 cups (250 grams) powdered sugar

1/4 cup (60 ml) heavy cream

Green food coloring (optional)

12 Oreos to decorate (optional)

Directions

1. Preheat your oven to 350°F (175°C) and line a muffin tin with cupcake liners.
2. In a large bowl, combine the flour, cocoa powder, sugar, baking powder, baking soda, and salt.
3. In another bowl, whisk together the eggs, milk, oil, vanilla extract, and mint extract.
4. Gradually add the wet ingredients to the dry ingredients, mixing until just combined.
5. Stir in the crushed Oreos.
6. Divide the batter evenly among the cupcake liners and bake for 20 minutes, or until a toothpick inserted into the center comes out clean.
7. While the cupcakes are cooling, prepare the frosting by beating the butter until creamy.
8. Gradually add the powdered sugar, beating until light and fluffy.
9. Beat in the heavy cream, mint extract, and a few drops of green food coloring, if using.
10. Once the cupcakes are completely cooled, frost them with the mint frosting.
11. Top each cupcake with an Oreo and enjoy!

There's nothing like the refreshing taste of mint paired with the rich, chocolatey goodness of Oreos. These mint Oreo cupcakes are the perfect treat for a summer picnic or a birthday party. Get ready to be the talk of the town, because these cupcakes are 'mint' to be shared!

blueberry lemon bliss cupcakes

YIELD: 12 CUPCAKES   BAKING TIME: 20-25 MIN

Ingredients

1 1/2 cups (190 grams) all-purpose flour

1 teaspoon baking powder

1/2 teaspoon baking soda

1/4 teaspoon salt

1 cup (200 grams) granulated sugar

1/2 cup (113 grams) unsalted butter, softened

2 large eggs

1 teaspoon pure vanilla extract

1 tablespoon lemon zest

1/2 cup (120 ml) milk

1 cup (150 grams) fresh blueberries

FOR THE FROSTING:

1 cup (226 grams) unsalted butter, softened

4 cups (500 grams) powdered sugar

1 tablespoon lemon juice

2 tablespoons milk

1/5 cup (75 grams) blueberries for decoration (optional)

Directions

1. Preheat your oven to 350°F (175°C) and line a muffin tin with cupcake liners.

2. In a medium bowl, whisk together the flour, baking powder, baking soda, and salt.

3. In a large bowl, beat the sugar and butter together until light and fluffy. Beat in the eggs, one at a time, followed by the vanilla extract and lemon zest.

4. Gradually add the dry ingredients to the butter mixture, alternating with the milk, beginning and ending with the dry ingredients. Gently fold in the blueberries.

5. Divide the batter evenly among the cupcake liners and bake for 20-25 minutes, or until a toothpick inserted into the center comes out clean.

6. While the cupcakes are cooling, prepare the frosting. Beat the butter until creamy, then gradually add the powdered sugar, lemon juice, and milk, beating until light and fluffy.

7. Once the cupcakes are completely cooled, frost them with the lemon buttercream and decorate with fresh blueberries. Enjoy!

There's nothing like the zesty tang of lemon paired with the sweet burst of blueberries to bring a smile to your face. These blueberry lemon bliss cupcakes are perfect for a summer picnic, a family gathering, or just a quiet afternoon with a good book. They're light, fluffy, and packed with flavor that will have everyone asking for seconds.

lovely vanilla rose cupcakes

YIELD: 12 CUPCAKES   BAKING TIME: 20-25 MIN

Ingredients

1 cup (200 grams) granulated sugar

1/2 cup (113 grams) unsalted butter, softened

2 large eggs

2 teaspoons vanilla extract

1 1/2 cups (190 grams) all-purpose flour

1 3/4 teaspoons baking powder

1/2 cup (120 ml) milk

1 tablespoon rose water

FOR THE FROSTING:

1/2 cup (113 grams) unsalted butter, softened

2 cups (250 grams) powdered sugar

1 teaspoon rose water

Pink food coloring (optional)

Directions

1. Preheat your oven to 350°F (175°C) and line a muffin tin with cupcake liners.

2. In a medium bowl, cream together the sugar and butter until light and fluffy.

3. Beat in the eggs, one at a time, then stir in the vanilla extract.

4. Combine the flour and baking powder, add to the creamed mixture and mix well.

5. Finally, stir in the milk and rose water until the batter is smooth.

6. Pour or spoon the batter into the prepared cupcake liners.

7. Bake for 20-25 minutes, or until a toothpick inserted into the center of a cupcake comes out clean.

8. While the cupcakes are cooling, make the frosting. Beat the butter until creamy, then gradually add the powdered sugar, rose water, and a few drops of pink food coloring if desired.

9. Once the cupcakes are completely cooled, frost them with the rose frosting.

There's nothing quite like the delicate, floral aroma of roses to set a romantic mood. These vanilla rose cupcakes are perfect for a cozy date night at home or a special occasion like Valentine's Day or an anniversary. Get ready to be whisked away to a world of elegance and decadence with every bite

snickers surprise cupcakes

Ingredients

1 cup (200 grams) granulated sugar
1/2 cup (113 grams) unsalted butter, softened
2 large eggs
1/3 cup (75 grams) unsweetened cocoa powder
1/2 teaspoon baking powder
1/4 teaspoon baking soda
1/4 teaspoon salt
1 1/2 cups (188 grams) all-purpose flour
3/4 cup (180 ml) milk
1 teaspoon vanilla extract
FOR THE FROSTING:
1/2 cup (113 grams) unsalted butter, softened
1/4 cup (60 ml) heavy cream
2 cups (250 grams) powdered sugar
1/2 cup (125 grams) creamy peanut butter
1/2 teaspoon vanilla extract
1/4 cup (60 grams) caramel sauce
2 chopped Snickers bars or crushed peanuts (to sprinkle)

Directions

1. Preheat your oven to 350°F (175°C) and line a muffin tin with cupcake liners.
2. In a large bowl, cream together the sugar and butter until light and fluffy. Beat in the eggs one at a time.
3. In a separate bowl, combine the cocoa powder, baking powder, baking soda, salt, and flour.
4. Gradually add the dry ingredients to the butter mixture, alternating with the milk. Stir in the vanilla extract.
5. Fill each cupcake liner 2/3 full with the batter. Bake for 20 minutes, or until a toothpick inserted into the center comes out clean. Allow the cupcakes to cool completely.
6. While the cupcakes are cooling, prepare the frosting. Beat together the butter, heavy cream, powdered sugar, peanut butter, and vanilla extract until smooth. Stir in the caramel sauce.
7. Once the cupcakes are cool, frost them with the peanut butter frosting. Top each cupcake with chopped Snickers bars or crushed peanuts.

Who doesn't love a good Snickers bar? Now imagine that in a cupcake form!
These Snickers cupcakes are the perfect treat for any occasion, but they're especially great
for birthday parties or game nights. They're a fun and delicious way to bring
a little bit of childhood nostalgia to your dessert table.

funfetti birthday blast cupcakes

YIELD: 12 CUPCAKES   BAKING TIME: 20 - 25 MIN

Ingredients

1 cup (200 grams) granulated sugar

1/2 cup (113 grams) unsalted butter, softened

2 eggs

2 teaspoons vanilla extract

1 1/2 cups (190 grams) all-purpose flour

1 3/4 teaspoons baking powder

1/2 cup (120 ml) milk

1/2 cup (80 grams) rainbow sprinkles

FOR THE FROSTING:

1/2 cup (113 grams) unsalted butter, softened

2 cups (250 grams) powdered sugar

1 teaspoons vanilla extract

2 tablespoons (30 ml) heavy cream

Extra sprinkles for decoration

Directions

1. Preheat your oven to 350°F (175°C) and line a muffin tin with cupcake liners.

2. In a large bowl, cream together the sugar and butter until light and fluffy. Beat in the eggs, one at a time, then stir in the vanilla.

3. Combine the flour and baking powder, add to the creamed mixture and mix well. Finally, stir in the milk until the batter is smooth. Fold in the sprinkles.

4. Pour or spoon the batter into the prepared muffin tin.

5. Bake for 20 to 25 minutes, or until a toothpick inserted into the center of a cupcake comes out clean. Allow to cool completely before frosting.

6. For the frosting, beat the butter until creamy. Gradually add the powdered sugar, vanilla, and heavy cream and beat until light and fluffy. Pipe or spread the frosting onto the cupcakes and top with extra sprinkles. Enjoy!

There's no better way to celebrate a birthday than with these funfetti birthday blast cupcakes. These cupcakes are a party in every bite, filled with colorful sprinkles that pop against the light, fluffy vanilla cake. They're perfect for kids' parties, but adults will love them too. After all, who doesn't love a little funfetti?

italian cannoli cupcakes

YIELD: 12 CUPCAKES   BAKING TIME: 20 MIN

Ingredients

1 1/2 cups (190 grams) all-purpose flour

1 1/2 teaspoons baking powder

1/4 teaspoon salt

1/2 cup (113 grams) unsalted butter, at room temperature

1 cup (200 grams) granulated sugar

2 large eggs

2 teaspoons pure vanilla extract

1/2 cup (120 ml) whole milk

FOR THE FROSTING:

2 cups (475 grams) ricotta cheese

1 cup (125 grams) powdered sugar

1 teaspoon pure vanilla extract

1/4 cup (60 grams) mini chocolate chips

Directions

1. Preheat your oven to 350°F (175°C) and line a muffin tin with cupcake liners.
2. In a medium bowl, whisk together the flour, baking powder, and salt.
3. In a large bowl, beat the butter and sugar together until light and fluffy. Beat in the eggs, one at a time, followed by the vanilla extract.
4. Gradually add the flour mixture to the butter mixture, alternating with the milk, beginning and ending with the flour mixture.
5. Divide the batter evenly among the cupcake liners and bake for 20 minutes, or until a toothpick inserted into the center of a cupcake comes out clean.
6. Allow the cupcakes to cool in the tin for 5 minutes, then transfer them to a wire rack to cool completely.
7. While the cupcakes are cooling, prepare the frosting. In a medium bowl, beat the ricotta cheese, powdered sugar, and vanilla extract together until smooth. Stir in the mini chocolate chips.
8. Once the cupcakes are completely cool, frost them with the ricotta frosting and sprinkle extra chocolate chips for decoration.

Inspired by the classic Italian dessert, these cannoli cupcakes with ricotta frosting are a delightful treat that will transport you straight to the heart of Italy. Perfect for a family gathering, a birthday party, or just a cozy afternoon tea, these cupcakes are sure to impress with their unique flavor and beautiful presentation.

biscoff cookie cupcakes

YIELD: 12 CUPCAKES   BAKING TIME: 20 MIN

Ingredients

1 1/2 cups (190 grams) all-purpose flour

1 1/2 teaspoons baking powder

1/2 teaspoon baking soda

1/4 teaspoon salt

1/2 cup (113 grams) unsalted butter, softened

1 cup (200 grams) granulated sugar

2 large eggs

2 teaspoons vanilla extract

3/4 cup (180 ml) buttermilk

1/2 cup (125 grams) Biscoff cookie spread

FOR THE FROSTING:

1/2 cup (113 grams) unsalted butter, softened

2 cups (250 grams) powdered sugar

1/2 cup (125 grams) Biscoff cookie spread

2 tablespoons (30 ml) heavy cream

1 teaspoon vanilla extract

Crushed Biscoff cookies for garnish

Directions

1. Preheat your oven to 350°F (175°C) and line a muffin tin with cupcake liners.

2. In a medium bowl, whisk together the flour, baking powder, baking soda, and salt.

3. In a large bowl, beat the butter and sugar together until light and fluffy. Beat in the eggs, one at a time, followed by the vanilla extract and Biscoff spread.

4. Gradually mix in the dry ingredients, alternating with the buttermilk, beginning and ending with the dry ingredients.

5. Divide the batter evenly among the cupcake liners and bake for 20 minutes, or until a toothpick inserted into the center comes out clean.

6. While the cupcakes are cooling, prepare the frosting. Beat the butter until creamy, then gradually beat in the powdered sugar. Mix in the Biscoff spread, heavy cream, and vanilla extract until smooth.

7. Once the cupcakes are completely cooled, frost them with the Biscoff frosting and garnish with crushed Biscoff cookies.

These Biscoff cookie cupcakes are a delightful treat that will transport you straight to cookie heaven. With a moist cupcake base infused with the unique flavors of Biscoff cookies, and topped with a creamy Biscoff frosting, you won't be able to resist indulging in one (or five) of these delectable creations.

rocky road cupcakes

YIELD: 12 CUPCAKES   BAKING TIME: 20-25 MIN

Ingredients

1 1/2 cups (190 grams) all-purpose flour

1/2 cup (50 grams) unsweetened cocoa powder

1 1/2 teaspoons baking powder

1/2 teaspoon baking soda

1/4 teaspoon salt

1 cup (200 grams) granulated sugar

1/2 cup (120 grams) unsalted butter, softened

2 large eggs

1 teaspoon vanilla extract

1 cup (240 ml) milk

1/2 cup (85 grams) chocolate chips

1/2 cup (60 grams) chopped nuts

1/2 cup (75 grams) mini marshmallows

FOR THE FROSTING:

1 cup (200 grams) granulated sugar

4 large egg whites

1/4 teaspoon cream of tartar

1 teaspoon vanilla extract

Directions

1. Preheat your oven to 350°F (175°C) and line a muffin tin with cupcake liners.

2. In a medium bowl, whisk together the flour, cocoa powder, baking powder, baking soda, and salt.

3. In a large bowl, beat the sugar and butter until light and fluffy. Beat in the eggs, one at a time, then stir in the vanilla.

4. Gradually add the flour mixture to the butter mixture, alternating with the milk, beginning and ending with the flour mixture. Stir in the nuts and marshmallows.

5. Divide the batter evenly among the cupcake liners and bake for 20-25 minutes, or until a toothpick inserted into the center comes out clean. Let the cupcakes cool completely.

6. For the frosting, combine the sugar, egg whites, and cream of tartar in a heatproof bowl set over a saucepan of simmering water. Whisk until the sugar is dissolved and the mixture is warm to the touch.

7. Remove the bowl from the heat and beat with an electric mixer on high speed until stiff, glossy peaks form. Beat in the vanilla.

8. Frost the cooled cupcakes with the marshmallow frosting and sprinkle with chocolate, nuts or marshmallows (optional).

Get ready to hit the sweetest road trip yet with these delectable rocky road cupcakes!
Packed with gooey marshmallows, crunchy nuts, and rich chocolate, these treats
will have you feeling like you've won the gold medal in dessert indulgence.
So buckle up and let your taste buds embark on a rocky (and utterly irresistible) adventure!

white chocolate raspberry cupcakes

YIELD: 12 CUPCAKES   BAKING TIME: 20 - 25 MIN

Ingredients

1/2 cup (113 grams) unsalted butter, softened

1 cup (200 grams) granulated sugar

2 large eggs

1 teaspoon vanilla extract

1 1/2 cups (180 grams) all-purpose flour

1 1/2 teaspoons baking powder

1/4 teaspoon salt

1/2 cup (120 ml) milk

1 cup (170 grams) white chocolate chips

1 cup (123 grams) fresh raspberries

FOR THE FROSTING:

1/2 cup (113 grams) unsalted butter, softened

2 cups (250 grams) powdered sugar

1 teaspoon vanilla extract

2 tablespoons (30 ml) milk

1/2 cup (85 grams) white chocolate chips, melted

Fresh raspberries for garnish

Directions

1. Preheat your oven to 350°F (175°C) and line a muffin tin with cupcake liners.

2. In a large bowl, cream together the butter and sugar until light and fluffy. Beat in the eggs, one at a time, followed by the vanilla extract.

3. In a separate bowl, combine the flour, baking powder, and salt. Gradually add this to the butter mixture, alternating with the milk. Stir in the white chocolate chips.

4. Gently fold in the raspberries, being careful not to crush them.

5. Divide the batter evenly among the cupcake liners and bake for 20 - 25 minutes, or until a toothpick inserted into the center comes out clean.

6. While the cupcakes are cooling, prepare the frosting. Beat the butter until creamy, then gradually add the powdered sugar, vanilla extract, and milk. Stir in the melted white chocolate.

7. Once the cupcakes are completely cooled, frost them with the white chocolate frosting and garnish with fresh raspberries. Enjoy!

Get ready to fall in love at first bite with these white chocolate raspberry cupcakes. A sweet tale of a cupcake that danced with a white chocolate and fell head over heels for a raspberry. It's a love story baked to perfection, and you're invited to the wedding!

thank you

As we come to the end of this delicious journey, I want to extend my heartfelt thanks to you for picking up this book and baking alongside me. I sincerely hope you've found joy in every recipe, every story, and every tip shared within these pages.

Baking is more than just a hobby or a skill—it's a form of expression, a labor of love. And sharing these recipes from my kitchen has been an absolute delight. Your decision to invest your time and effort into bringing these recipes to life means the world to me.

I want to encourage you to keep experimenting and keep baking. Don't be afraid to add your own personal touch to the recipes or to try new flavors. After all, baking is an adventure, and every adventure is uniquely your own.

Lastly, if you've enjoyed this book and found the recipes tasty and the tips helpful, I would be truly grateful if you could take a few minutes to leave a review. Your feedback not only helps me improve, but it also helps fellow bakers find this book.

Thank you once again for joining me in this baking adventure. Here's to many more sweet moments and delicious treats to come!

Linda

Printed in Great Britain
by Amazon